Discipline
with Love

○ ○ ○

A Tyndale Treasure by
DR. JAMES DOBSON

Tyndale House
Publishers, Inc.
Wheaton, Illinois

Discipline with Love is adapted from
Dare to Discipline by Dr. James Dobson,
copyright © 1970 by Tyndale House Publishers,
Wheaton Illinois.
Library of Congress Catalog Card Number 72-84424
ISBN 0-8423-0665-X
Printed in the United States of America.

05 04 03 02 01

33 32 31 30 29

TEACHING RESPECT AND RESPONSIBILITY TO CHILDREN

Nature has generously equipped most animals with a fear of things that could be harmful to them. Their survival depends on recognition of a particular danger in time to avoid it. But good old mother nature did not protect the frog quite so well; she overlooked a serious flaw in his early warning system that sometimes proves fatal. If a frog is placed in a pan of warm water under which the heat is being increased very gradually, he will typically show no inclination to escape. Since he is a cold-blooded creature, his body temperature remains approximately the same as the water around him and he does not notice the slow change taking place. As the temperature continues to intensify, the frog remains oblivious to his danger; he could easily hop his way to safety, but he is apparently thinking about something else. He will just sit there, contentedly peering over the edge of the pan while the steam curls ominously around his nostrils. Eventually, the boiling frog will pass on to his reward, having succumbed to an unnecessary misfortune that he could easily have avoided.

Now obviously, this is a book about parents and

1

children, not frogs. But human beings have some of the same perceptual inadequacies as their little green friends. We quickly become excited about *sudden* dangers that confront us. War, disease, epidemics, earthquakes, and hurricanes bring instant mobilization. However, if a threatening problem arises very slowly, perhaps over a decade or two, we often allow ourselves to "boil" in happy ignorance. This blindness to gradual disasters is best illustrated by the way we have ignored the turmoil that is spreading systematically through the younger generation of Americans. We have passively accepted a slowly deteriorating "youth scene" without uttering a croak of protest. Suppose the parents of yesterday could make a brief visit to our world to observe the conditions that prevail among our children; certainly, they would be dismayed and appalled by the juvenile problems which have been permitted to become widespread (and are spreading wider) in urban America.

Narcotic and drug usage by America's juveniles is an indescribable shame. Although the danger is now getting wide publicity, the adult who has not worked with teen-agers recently may be unaware of the degree to which this activity has infiltrated adolescent society in the past few years. In 1960 there were 1,500 juvenile arrests for narcotics usage in the State of California; in 1968 there were 30,000. That is an increase of 2,000 percent in an eight-year period. The magnitude of the problem was further described in the following quotation, taken from a recent article in *Time* magazine:

"A heroin epidemic has hit us. We must face that fact," says Dr. Donald Louria, president of the New York State Council on Drug Addiction and author of *Drug Scene*. Dr. Elliot Luby, associate director of Detroit's addict-treating Lafayette Clinic, concurs: "Addiction is really reaching epidemic proportions. You have to look at it as an infectious disease." Epidemic, of course, is a relative term, but as a Chicago psychiatrist, Dr. Marvin Schwarz, says: "Now we're seeing it clinically, whereas before we weren't. The kids on heroin all have long histories of drug use." At the California-based Synanon self-help centers for addicts, the teen-age population has risen from zero five years ago to 400 today. In San Francisco, Dr. Barry Ramer, director of the Study for Special Problems, calls heroin now "the most readily available drug on the streets." He adds: "In my wildest nightmares, I never dreamed of what we are seeing today."[1]

Many young people are now playing another dangerous game, packaged neatly under the title of sexual freedom. The rationale sounds very plausible: why should you be restricted by the hangups of the past generation? Why shouldn't you enjoy this greatest of life's pleasures? Now that God is dead, who has the authority to deny you this fulfillment? Contraceptives will prevent babies, so why not find out what everyone is talking about? Now certainly, illicit sex is not a new phenomenon; this activity has been with us for a few thousand years. How-

[1]*Time* magazine, March 16, 1970, p. 16. Used by permission.

3

ever, immorality has never been embraced as right and proper in America until now. "Bed today, wed tomorrow—maybe" is the plea. Without being unnecessarily pessimistic, it is accurate to say that the traditional concept of morality is *dead* among the majority of high school students today. The "Playboy Philosophy" has been accepted as the banner of the now generation. I spoke recently to a group of high school homemaking teachers who related their surprise at the blatant admission of immorality by their students. Whole classes now argue with their teachers about the "rightness" of sexual freedom.

The casualties of this permissive sexual philosophy have been known for centuries and can hardly be overlooked today: (1) Illegitimate pregnancies and their accompanying heartache are common in most high schools in this country. (2) Venereal disease has reached epidemic proportions within the cities. A physician who directs a venereal disease clinic recently described for me the depressing conditions he witnesses. He said most of his young patients do not come wringing their hands in despair at the awful disease they have contracted; rather, they schedule routine visits to his clinic in order to "cure" what they carry in time for the events of the next weekend! The medical examination serves as a pit stop for their upcoming exploits. (3) Perhaps the most severe result of promiscuity is the effect it has on the emotions and personality, subjecting innocence and wholesomeness to an untimely death. These consequences of sexual permissiveness are not widely advertised by the advocates of the new morality!

Another symptom of the adolescent unrest is seen in the frequent display of aggression and hostility. Young people are more violent today than at any period in American history. According to published FBI figures, juvenile arrests for aggravated assault have increased seventy percent faster than the general population in recent years. Two-thirds of all the crimes of violence (murder, rape, and assault) are committed by those under twenty-one years of age. A recent Associated Press article stated that students across the United States are attacking their teachers with increasing frequency. Most of these physical attacks occur in the junior and senior high schools, although a surprising number of the episodes take place at the elementary school level. Can there be any doubt that school authority is being challenged seriously?

There are many related phenomena occurring among the young which reveal the turmoil in adolescent society. Emotional maladjustment, gang warfare, teen-age suicide, school failure, shoplifting, and grand larceny are symptoms of a deeper illness that plague vast numbers of America's young. During the earlier days of the adolescent rebellion, the reassuring watchword was "only a small percentage of the youngsters are getting into trouble." That statement no longer comforts us, because it is no longer true. On the other hand, it would be grossly unfair to say that most young people are "bad"; they are merely responding to social forces and causes that are leading them into the icy face of disaster.

We cannot solve these problems by lashing out at the young with venom and hostility. Many of the

5

youngsters who are behaving in such antisocial and self-destructive ways are actually lost, aimless, and valueless individuals. Millions of other teen-agers have not attacked society or rejected its time-honored values, yet they experience the same inner emptiness and confusion. They are badly in need of wise and understanding parents who can anchor them during their personal crises. Certainly, the purpose of this book is not to condemn our children; they are our most important and valued resource. To the contrary, the older generation must assume the blame for allowing the circumstances to deteriorate. There was a time when the trend could easily have been reversed, but like the contented frog, we must have been thinking about something else. The time has come for us to hop, rather than boil. It is our parental responsibility to get off our corpulent behinds and take steps to eliminate the problems which threaten our children. We may not salvage some members of the present generation but perhaps we can preserve the next. Ultimately, we must deal with this question: how did we get into this mess and how can we get out of it?

Without meaning to oversimplify a very complicated picture, it is accurate to say that many of our difficulties with the present generation of young people began in the tender years of their childhood. Little children are exceedingly vulnerable to the teaching (good or bad) of their guardians, and mistakes made in the early years prove costly, indeed. There is a critical period during the first four or five years of a child's life when he can be taught proper attitudes. These early concepts become rather permanent. When the opportunity of those years is missed, however, the prime receptivity usually vanishes, never to return. If it is desirable that children be kind, appreciative, and pleasant, those qualities should be taught—not hoped for. If we want to see honesty, truthfulness, and unselfishness in our offspring, then these characteristics should be the conscious objectives of our early instructional process. If it is important to produce respectful, responsible young citizens, then we should set out to mold them accordingly. The point is obvious: *heredity does not equip a child with proper attitudes; children will learn what they are taught.* We cannot expect the desirable attitudes and behavior to appear if we have not done our early homework. It seems clear that many of the parents of the post-war crop of American babies failed in that critical assignment.

Nature is rather careless about whom it allows to become mammas and papas. The qualifications are not very high; in fact, it is not necessary to know a single fact about children in order to produce one. Young men and women may find themselves saddled with the unwanted responsibility for impressionable, helpless infants, about whom they know nothing. They may be totally ignorant of the principles of discipline, nutrition, or child growth and development. The mistakes that they make are certainly unintentional, yet the consequences are no less severe.

At a recent psychologists' conference in Los Angeles, the keynote speaker made the statement that *the greatest social disaster of this century is the belief that abundant love makes discipline unnecessary.* He said that some of the little terrors who are unmanageable in the school classroom are *mistakenly* believed to have emotional problems. They are referred to the school psychologist for his evaluation of their difficulty, but no deep problems are found. Instead, it becomes obvious that the children have simply never been required to inhibit their behavior or restrict their impulses. Some of these children came from homes where love was almost limitless.

Respectful and responsible children result from families where the proper combination of *love and discipline* is present. Both these ingredients must be applied in the necessary quantities. An absence of either is often disastrous. During the 1950s, an unfortunate imbalance existed, when we saw the predominance of a happy theory called "permissive democracy." This philosophy minimized parental obligations to control their children, in some cases making mom and dad feel that all forms of punishment were harmful and unfair. As a result, the mid-century decade has been described as the most permissive ten years in our history. Is it merely coincidental that the generation raised during that era has grown up to challenge every form of authority that confronts it? I think not. It should come as no surprise that our beloved children have hangups; we have sacrificed this generation on the altar of overindulgence, permissiveness, and smother-love.

Have you considered the fact that the present generation of young people has enjoyed more of the "good life" than any comparable group in the history of the world? One can define the good life any way he chooses; the conclusion remains the same. Our children have had more pleasure and entertainment, better food, more leisure time, better education, better medicine, more material goods, and more opportunities than has ever been known before.

The central cause of the turmoil among the young must be found in the tender years of childhood: we demanded neither respect nor responsible behavior from our children, and it should not be surprising that some of our young citizens are now demonstrating the absence of these virtues.

○ ○ ○

A SHORT ESSAY ON
CHILD DISCIPLINE

Methods and philosophies regarding control of children have been the subject of heated debate and disagreement for centuries. The pendulum has swept back and forth regularly between harsh, oppressive discipline and the unstructured permissiveness of the 1950s. It is time that we realize that *both* extremes leave their characteristic scars on the lives of young victims, and I would be hard pressed to say which is more damaging. Unfortunately, the prevailing philosophy at a particular time seems to be more influential on parental approaches to discipline than does common sense. For example, I know of one mother who spanks her six-month-old baby for not lying still while being diapered. Many such foolish examples of repressive discipline are easily observable in our society. However, the opposite is still more prevalent.

The American public has been subjected to many wild-horse opinions about child discipline, which have galloped off rapidly in all directions. Everyone from Aunt Bessie to the local undertaker has his own unique viewpoint about how children should be controlled, and what is worse, the experts have often been in direct contradiction with one another. The cause of their disagreement is simple: the principles of good discipline cannot be ascertained by scientific inquiry. The subject is too complicated and there are too many variables involved. Despite this disagreement in the past, I am thoroughly convinced that the proper control of children can be found in a reasonable, common sense philosophy, where five key elements are paramount.

1. *Developing respect for the parents is the critical factor in child management.* It is most important that a child respect his parents, not for the purpose of satisfying their egos, but because the child's relationship with his parents provides the basis for his attitude toward all other people. His view of parental authority becomes the cornerstone of his later outlook on school authority, police and law, the people with whom he will eventually live and work, and for society in general. The parent-child relationship is the first and most important social interaction an infant will have, and the flaws and knots in that interaction can often be seen in later relationships. For example, suppose a child wants some candy but his parents refuse, so he falls down on the floor and screams and bangs his head on the carpet. Mamma then becomes upset by the display and says, "Here, Johnny, I guess one piece of candy won't hurt you. Now stop crying." She has made it profitable for Johnny to react emotionally. His yelling paid a tasty dividend. He challenged the system and won the battle. If good-hearted mom follows that same approach to his protests during

11

the next fourteen years, little Johnny may gradually grow up to become Big Bad John, expecting everyone else to yield to his demands as his weak old mamma did. When rebuffed later by a less pliable authority, the stage is set for a violent collision. Although this example is deliberately oversimplified, I could give many similar illustrations which would show how the early parent-child relationship is reflected in later human interaction.

Respect for the parent must be maintained for another equally important reason. If you want your child to accept your values when he reaches his teen years, then you must be worthy of his respect during his younger days. When a child can successfully defy his parents during his first fifteen years, laughing in their faces and stubbornly flouting their authority, he develops a natural contempt for them. "Stupid old Mom and Dad! I've got them wound around my little finger. Sure they love me, but I really think they're afraid of me." A child may not utter these words, but he feels them each time he outsmarts his adult companions and wins the confrontations and battles. Later he is likely to demonstrate his disrespect in a more open manner. His parents are not deserving of his respect, and he does not want to identify with anything they represent. He rejects every vestige of their philosophy. This factor is important for Christian parents who wish to sell their concept of God to their children. They must first sell themselves. If they are not worthy of respect, then neither is their religion or their morals, or their government, or their country, or any of their values. This becomes the "genera-

tion gap" at its most basic level. The chasm
not develop from a failure to communicate; we're
speaking approximately the same language. Our
difficulties between generations result more from
what we *do* understand in our communication than
in our confusion with words. The conflict between
generations occurs because of a breakdown in mu-
tual respect, and it bears many painful consequences.

The issue of respect can be a useful tool in knowing when to punish and how excited one should get
about a given behavior. First, the parent should
decide whether an undesirable behavior represents
a direct challenge of his authority—to his position
as the father or mother. Punishment should depend
on that evaluation. For example, suppose little
Walter is acting silly in the living room, and he falls
into a table, breaking many expensive china cups
and other trinkets. Or suppose he loses his bicycle
or leaves Dad's best saw out in the rain. These are
acts of childish irresponsibility and should be
handled as such. Perhaps the parent should have
the child work to pay for the losses—depending on
the age and maturity of the child, of course. However, these examples do not constitute direct chal-
lenges to authority. They do not emanate from
willful, haughty disobedience. In my opinion,
spankings should be reserved for the moment a
child (age ten or less) expresses a defiant "I will
not!" or "You shut up!" When a youngster tries
this kind of stiff-necked rebellion, you had better
take it out of him, and pain is a marvelous purifier.
When nose-to-nose confrontation occurs between

13

you and your child, it is not the time to have a discussion about the virtues of obedience. It is not the occasion to send him in his room to pout. It is not appropriate to wait until poor, tired old dad comes plodding in from work, just in time to handle the conflicts of the day. You have drawn a line in the dirt, and the child has deliberately flopped his big hairy toe across it. Who is going to win? Who has the most courage? Who is in charge here? If you do not answer these questions conclusively for the child, he will precipitate other battles designed to ask them again and again. It is the ultimate paradox of childhood that a youngster wants to be controlled, but he insists that his parents earn the right to control him.

Much sound advice has been written about the dangers of inappropriate discipline, and it should be heeded. A parent can absolutely destroy a child through the application of harsh, oppressive, whimsical, unloving, and/or capricious punishment. I am certainly not recommending such. However, you cannot inflict permanent damage to a child if you follow this technique: identify the rules well in advance; let there be no doubt about what is and is not acceptable behavior; when the child cold-bloodedly chooses to challenge those known boundaries in a haughty manner, give him good reason to regret it; at all times, demonstrate love and affection and kindness and understanding. *Discipline and love are not antithetical;* one is a function of the other. The parent must convince himself that punishment (as outlined above) is not something he does *to* the child; it is something he

14

does *for* the child. His attitude towards his disobedient youngster is this, "I love you too much to let you behave like that."

Respect is unsuccessful as a unilateral affair; it must operate on a *two-way* street. A mother cannot require her child to treat her with dignity if she will not do the same for him. She should be gentle with his ego, never belittling him or embarrassing him in front of his friends. Punishment should usually be administered away from the curious eyes of gloating onlookers. The child should not be laughed at unmercifully. His strong feelings and requests, even if foolish, should be given an honest appraisal. He should feel that his parents "really *do* care about me." Self-esteem is the most fragile attribute in human nature; it can be damaged by a very minor incident and its reconstruction is often difficult to engineer. A father who is sarcastic and biting in his criticism of children cannot expect to receive genuine respect in return. His offspring might *fear* him enough to conceal their contempt, but revenge will often erupt in late adolescence.

A mother can expect her child to challenge her authority regularly from the time he is about fifteen months of age, if not earlier. The toddler is the world's most hard-nosed opponent of law and order, and he can make life miserable for his harassed mom. In his own innocent way, he is vicious and selfish and demanding and cunning and destructive. Comedian Bill Cosby must have had some personal losses at the hands of a toddler; he is quoted as saying, "Give me 200 active two-year-olds and I can conquer the world." The child be-

15

tween fifteen and thirty months of age does not want to be restricted or inhibited in any manner and he is not inclined to conceal his viewpoint. He resents every nap imposed on him, and bedtime becomes an exhausting ordeal to be dreaded. He wants to play with everything he sees, particularly fragile and expensive ornaments. He prefers using his pants rather than the potty, and he insists on eating with his hands. When he breaks loose in a store, he invariably runs as fast as his fat little legs will carry him. He picks up the kitty by her ears, and then screams in protest when he gets scratched. He wants his mamma to be within three feet of him all day long, preferably serving as his full-time playmate. Truly, the toddler is a tiger! Even if his parents do everything right in disciplining him, they are still likely to find him hard to control. For this reason, they should not hope to make their two-year-old act like an adult. A controlling but patient hand will eventually succeed in settling the little tyrant, but probably not until he is about four years of age. Unfortunately, however, the child's attitude toward authority can be severely damaged during his toddler years. The parent who loves her cute little butterball so much that she cannot risk antagonizing him, may lose and never regain his control.

When a parent loses the early confrontations with the child, the later conflicts become harder to win. The parent who never wins, who is too weak or too tired or too busy to win, is making a costly mistake that will come back to haunt him during the child's adolescence. If you can't make a

16

five-year-old pick up his toys, it is unlikely that you will exercise any impressive degree of control during his adolescence, the most defiant time of life. It is important to understand that adolescence is a condensation or composite of all the training and behavior that has gone before. Any unsettled matter in the first twelve years is likely to fester and erupt during adolescence. The proper time to begin disarming the teen-age time-bomb is twelve years before it arrives.

I must point out the fact that some rebellious behavior is distinctly different in origin from the "challenging" defiance I've been describing. A child's antagonism and stiff-lipped negativism may emanate from frustration, disappointment, or rejection, and must be interpreted as a warning signal to be heeded. Perhaps the toughest task in parenthood is to recognize the difference between these two distinct motives. A child's resistant behavior always contains a message to his parents which they must decode before responding. That message is often phrased in the form of a question: "Are you in charge or am I?" A forceful reply is appropriate to that query as a discouragement to his future attempts to overthrow constituted government in the home. On the other hand, Junior's antagonism may be saying, "I feel unloved now that I'm stuck with that yelling baby brother. Mom used to care for me; now nobody wants me. I hate everybody." When this kind of meaning underlies the rebellion, the parents should move quickly to pacify its cause. The most successful parents are those who have the skill to get behind the eyes of

17

the child, seeing what he sees, thinking what he thinks, feeling what he feels. Unless they can master this ability, they will continually react in a harmful manner. For example, when a two-year-old screams and cries at bedtime, one must ascertain what he is communicating. If he is genuinely frightened by the blackness of his room, the appropriate response should be quite different than if he is merely protesting about having to go nighty-night. The art of good parenthood revolves around the interpretation of meaning behind behavior.

Repeating the first point, the most vital objective of disciplining a child is to gain and maintain his respect. If the parents fail in this task, life becomes complicated, indeed.

2. *The best opportunity to communicate often occurs after punishment.* Nothing brings a parent and child closer together than for the mother or father to win decisively after being defiantly challenged. This is particularly true if the child was "asking for it," knowing full well that he deserved what he got. The parent's demonstration of his authority builds respect like no other process, and the child will often reveal his affection when the emotion has passed. For this reason, the parent should not dread or shrink back from these confrontations with the child. These occasions should be anticipated as important events, because they provide the opportunity to say something to the child that cannot be said at other times. It is not necessary to beat the child into submission; a little bit of pain goes a long way for a young child. However, the spanking

should be of sufficient magnitude to cause the child to cry genuinely. After the emotional ventilation, the child will often want to crumple to the breast of his parent, and he should be welcomed with open, warm, loving arms. At that moment you can talk heart to heart. You can tell him how much you love him, and how important he is to you. You can explain why he was punished and how he can avoid the difficulty next time. This kind of communication is not made possible by other disciplinary measures, including standing the child in the corner or taking away his firetruck.

I was attempting to teach the art of good discipline to the mother of a fifteen-month-old girl, and she related an incident to me which illustrates the desired outcome. Suzie decided she didn't want to mind her mother, Mrs. Butler, when told not to run out the back door. It was sprinkling and Mrs. Butler did not want her to go outside because she was barefoot. Suzie's mother went out to get some firewood and told her to wait in the doorway. The child knew the meaning of the command because she learned to talk quite early; nevertheless, she came toddling across the patio. Mrs. Butler caught her and took her back, giving the same order more sternly. As soon as her back was turned, Suzie ran out again. On the third trip, her mother stung her little legs a few times with a switch. After the tears had subsided, Mrs. Butler was putting the firewood in the fireplace when Suzie came to her and reached out her arms, saying "Love, mommie." She gathered her child tenderly in her arms, of course, and rocked her for fifteen minutes, talking softly about the importance of obedience.

Parental warmth after punishment is essential to demonstrate to the child that it was his behavior, and not the child himself, that the parent rejected. William Glasser, the father of Reality Therapy, made this distinction very clear when he described the difference between discipline and punishment. "Discipline" is directed at the objectionable behavior, and the child will accept its consequences without resentment. By contrast, he defined punishment as a response that is directed at the individual. As such it is deeply resented by the child; punishment is the parent's personal thrust at the child; it is a desire of one person to hurt another; it is an expression of hostility rather than corrective love. When authorities talk about the emotional dangers of corporal punishment (spanking), they fail to discriminate between these two important approaches. Although Glasser's definition of the term punishment has not been applied throughout this book, the concept he has conveyed is of the greatest importance. Unquestionably, there is a wrong way to correct a child, and a major recurring error at this point can make a youngster feel unloved, unwanted, and insecure. One of the best guarantees against these misinterpretations is a loving conclusion to the disciplinary session.

3. *Control without nagging (It is possible).* Yelling and nagging at children can become a habit, and an ineffectual one at that! Have you ever screamed at your child, "This is the last time I'm going to tell you, 'this is that last time' "? Parents often use anger to get action, instead of using action to get action. It doesn't work. Let me give you an example.

Eight-year-old Henry is sitting on the floor, playing with his games. Mom looks at her watch and says, "Henry, it's nearly nine o'clock (a thirty-minute exaggeration) so gather up your junk and go take your bath." Now Henry knows, and Mom knows, that she doesn't mean for him to go take a bath. She merely meant for him to start *thinking* about going to take his bath. She would have fainted dead away if he had responded to her empty command. Approximately ten minutes later, Mom speaks again, "Now, Henry, it is getting later and you have to go to school tomorrow, and I want those toys picked up; then go get in that tub!" She still does not intend for Henry to obey, and he knows it. Her *real* message is "We're getting closer, Hank." Henry shuffles around and stacks a box or two to demonstrate that he heard her. Then he settles down for a few more minutes of play. Six minutes pass, and Mom issues another command, this time with more passion and threat in her voice, "Now listen, young man, I told you to get a move on, and I meant it." To Henry, this means he must get his toys picked up and meander toward the bathroom door. If his mom pursues him with a rapid step, then he must carry out the assignment posthaste. However, if Mom's mind wanders before she performs the last step of this ritual, Henry is free to enjoy a few more seconds reprieve.

You see, Henry and his mom are involved in a one-act play; they both know the rules and the role being enacted by the opposite player. The entire scene is programmed, computerized, and scripted. Whenever Mom wants Henry to do something he dislikes, she progresses through graduated steps of phony anger, beginning with calm and ending with a red flush and a threat. Henry does not have to move until she reaches the peak anger point. How foolish this game is! Since Mom controls him by the use of empty threats she has to stay mad all the time. Her relationship with her children is contaminated, and she ends each day with a pounding, throbbing headache. She can never count on instant obedience; it takes her at least five minutes to work up a believable degree of anger.

How much better it is to use *action* to get action. There are hundreds of tools which will bring the desired response. Minor pain can provide excellent motivation for the child. The parent should have some means of making the child want to cooperate, other than simply obeying because he was told to do so. For those who can think of no such device, I will suggest one: there is a muscle, lying snugly against the base of the neck. Anatomy books list it as the trapezius muscle, and when firmly squeezed, it sends little messengers to the brain saying, "This hurts; avoid recurrence at all costs." The pain is only temporary; it can cause no damage. When the youngster ignores being told to do something by his parent, he should know that Mom has a practical recourse. Let's return to the bedtime issue between Henry and his Mom; she should have told him that he had fifteen more minutes to play. It then would have been wise to set the alarm clock or the stove buzzer to sound in fifteen minutes. No one, child or adult, likes a sudden interruption to his activity. When the time came, Mom should have quietly told Henry to go take his bath. If he didn't move immediately, the shoulder muscle could have been squeezed. If Henry learns that this procedure is invariably followed, he will move before the consequence is applied.

There will be those among my readers who feel that the deliberate, premeditated application of minor pain to a sweet little child is a harsh and unloving recommendation. I ask those skeptics to hear me out. Consider the alternatives. On the one hand, there is constant nagging and strife between parent and child. When the youngster discovers there is no threat behind the millions of words he hears, he stops listening to them. The only messages he responds to are those reaching a peak of emotion, which means there is much screaming and yelling going on. The child is pulling in the opposite direction, fraying Mom's nerves and straining the parent-child relationship. But the most important limitation of these verbal reprimands is that their user often has to resort to physical punishment in the end, anyway. Thus, instead of the discipline being administered in a calm and judicious manner, the parent has become unnerved and frustrated, swinging wildly at the belligerent child. There was no reason for a fight to have occurred. The situation could have ended very differently if the parental attitude had been one of confident serenity. Speaking softly, almost pleasantly, Mom says, "Henry, you know what happens when you don't mind me; now I don't see any reason in the world why I should have to make you feel pain to get your cooperation tonight, but if you insist, I'll play the game with you. When the buzzer sounds you let me know what your decision is." The child has a choice to make, and the advantages to him of obeying his mother's wishes are clear. She need not scream. She need not threaten to shorten his life. She need not become upset. She is in command. Of course, Mother will have to prove two or three times that she will apply the pain, if necessary, and occasionally throughout the coming months her child will check to see if she is still at the helm. But there is no question in my mind as to which of these two approaches involves the least pain and the least hostility between parent and child.

Discipline in a school classroom is not very different from discipline at home; the principles by which children can be controlled are the same in both settings—only the methods change. A teacher, scoutmaster, or recreatioin leader who tries to control a group of children by use of his own anger is due for a long, long day of frustration. The children find out how far he will go before taking any action, and they invariably push him right to that line. Perhaps the most nonsensical mistake a teacher or group leader can make is to impose disciplinary measures that the children do not dislike. I knew a teacher, for example, who would scream and yell and beg her class to cooperate. When they got completely out of hand, she resorted to her maximum firepower: she would climb up on her desk and blow her whistle! The kids loved it! She weighed about 240 pounds, and the children would plot at the lunch and recess periods as to how they could get her on that desk. She was inadvertently offering them a reward for their unruliness. Their attitude was much like that of Brer Rabbit who begged the fox not to throw him in the briar patch. There was nothing they wanted more.

One should never underestimate a child's awareness that he is breaking the rules. I think most children are rather analytical about their defiance of adult authority; they consider the deed in advance, weighing its probable consequences. If the odds are too great that justice will triumph, they'll take a safer course. This characteristic is verified in millions of homes where the youngster will push one parent to the limits of his tolerance, but will be a sweet angel with the other. Mom whimpers, "Rick minds his dad perfectly, but he won't pay any attention to me." Good old Rick has observed that mom is safer than dad.

4. *Don't saturate the child with excessive materialism.* Despite the hardships of the Great Depression, at least one question was then easier to answer than it is today; how can I say "no" to my child's materialistic desires? It was very simple for parents to tell their children that they couldn't afford to buy them everything they wanted; dad could barely keep bread on the table. But in the opulent times, the parental task becomes more difficult. It takes considerably more courage to say, "No, I *won't* buy you Baby-Blow-Her-Nose," than it did to say, "I'm sorry, but you know we can't afford to buy that doll." The child's lust for expensive toys is carefully gen-

erated through millions of dollars spent on TV advertising by toy manufacturers. The commercials are skillfully made so that the toys look like full-sized copies of their real counterparts: jet airplanes, robot monsters, and automatic rifles. The little buyer sits open-mouthed in utter fascination. Five minutes later he begins a campaign that will eventually cost his dad $14.95 plus batteries and tax. The trouble is, Dad *can* afford to buy the new item, if not with cash, at least with his magic credit card. And when three other children on the block get the coveted toys, Mom and Dad begin to feel the pressure, and even the guilt. They feel selfish because they have indulged themselves for similar luxuries. Suppose the parents are courageous enough to resist the child's urging; the child is not blocked—grandparents are notoriously easy to "con." Even if the child is unsuccessful in getting his parents or grandparents to buy what he wants, there is an annual, foolproof resource: Santa Claus! When junior asks Santa to bring him something, his parents are in an inescapable trap. What can they say, "Santa can't afford it!"? Is Santa going to forget and disappoint him? No, the toy will be on Santa's sleigh.

Some would ask, "And why not? Why shouldn't we let our children enjoy the fruits of our good times?" Certainly I would not deny the child a reasonable quantity of the things he craves. But many American children are inundated with excesses that work toward their detriment. It has been said that prosperity offers a greater test of character than does adversity, and I'm inclined to agree. There are few conditions that inhibit a sense of appreciation more than for a child to feel he is entitled to whatever he wants, whenever he wants it. It is enlightening to watch as a child tears open stacks of presents at his birthday party or perhaps at Christmas time. One after another, the expensive contents are tossed aside with little more than a glance. The child's mother is made uneasy by this lack of enthusiasm and appreciation, so she says, "Oh, Marvin! Look what it is! It's a little tape recorder! What do you say to Grandmother? Give Grandmother a big hug. Did you hear me, Marvin? Go give Grams a big hug and kiss." Marvin may or may not choose to make the proper noises to Grandmother. His lack of exuberance results from the fact that prizes which are won cheaply are of little value, regardless of the cost to the original purchaser.

There is another reason that the child should be denied some of the things he thinks he wants. Although it sounds paradoxical, you actually cheat him of pleasure when you give him too much. Pleasure occurs when an intense need is satisfied. If there is no need, there is no pleasure. A glass of water is worth more than gold to a man dying of thirst. The analogy to children should be obvious. If you never allow a child to want something, he never enjoys the pleasure of receiving it. If you buy him a tricycle before he can walk, and a bicycle before he can ride, and a car before he can drive, and a diamond ring before he knows the value of money, he accepts these gifts with little pleasure and less appreciation. How unfortunate that such a child never had the chance to long for something,

27

dreaming about it at night and plotting for it by day. He might have even gotten desperate enough to work for it. The same possession that brought a yawn could have been a trophy and a treasure. I suggest that you allow your child the thrill of temporary deprivation; it's more fun and *much* less expensive.

5. *Avoid extremes in control* and *love.* There is little question about the consequences of disciplinary extremes. On the side of harshness, a child suffers the humiliation of total domination. The atmosphere is icy and rigid, and he lives in constant fear. He is unable to make his own decisions and his personality is squelched beneath the hobnailed boot of parental authority. Lasting characteristics of dependency, overwhelming hostility, and psychosis can emerge from this overbearing oppression. The opposite position, ultimate permissiveness, is equally tragic. Under this setting, the child is his own master from his earliest babyhood. He thinks the world revolves around his heady empire, and he often has utter contempt and disrespect for those closest to him. Anarchy and chaos reign in his home, and his mother is often the most nervous, frustrated woman on her block. When the child is young, the mother is stranded at home because she is too embarrassed to take her little devil anywhere. It would be worth enduring the hardships if this confusion produced healthy, secure children. Unfortunately the child usually suffers the most difficulties from such anarchistic circumstances. This book began by emphasizing the hazards and social

consequences of the extreme permissive approach to child rearing. But if there is anything I don't want to do, it is to cause parents to overreact, committing the opposite sin. Both extremes are disastrous. There is safety only in the middle ground, which is sometimes difficult to locate.

Extreme degrees of love can also be unhealthy for a child. The complete absence of love (rejection) will destroy him emotionally, and in some cases physically. It has been known for several decades that an infant who is not loved, touched, and caressed will often die. Evidence of this fact was observed as early as the thirteenth century, when Frederick II conducted an experiment with fifty infants. He wanted to see what language the children would speak if they never had the opportunity to hear the spoken word. To accomplish this dubious research project, he assigned foster mothers to bathe and suckle the children, but forbade them to fondle, pet, or talk to their charges. The experiment failed because all fifty infants died. Hundreds of more recent studies indicate that the mother-child relationship during the first year of life is apparently vital to the infant's survival. An unloved child is truly the saddest phenomenon in all of nature.

While the absence of love has a predictable effect on children, it is not so well known that excessive love or "super love" has its hazards, too. Even some venerable experts, like Dr. Karl Menninger, do not acknowledge the dangers of excessive parental affection. Despite my respect for Dr. Menninger, I must disagree with his view that no child has ever been spoiled by love, and that a spoiled child is one who has been neglected by being ignored, or has been terrorized by threats of retribution for his mischief or has been bribed by indulgence. I believe some children *are* spoiled by love. Americans are tremendously child-oriented at this stage in their history; many parents have invested all of their hopes, dreams, desires, and ambitions in their youngsters. The natural culmination of this philosophy is overprotection of the next generation. I dealt with one anxious parent who stated that her children were the *only* sources of her satisfaction. During the long summers, she spent most of her time sitting at the front room window, watching her three girls while they played. She feared that they might get hurt or need her assistance; or they might ride their bikes in the street. Her responsibilities to her husband were sacrificed, despite his vigorous complaints. She did not have time to clean her house; guard duty at the window was her only function. She suffered enormous tensions over the known and unknown threats that could destroy her beloved offspring.

Childhood illness and sudden danger are always difficult for a loving parent to tolerate, but the slightest threat produces unbearable anxiety for the overprotective mom and dad. Unfortunately, the overprotective parent is not the only one who suffers; the child is often its victim, too. It has been theorized that asthma is more likely to occur in a "smother-loved" child, although the relationship has not been established conclusively. Other consequences of overprotection are less speculative.

The overprotective parent finds it difficult to allow her child to take reasonable risks; those risks are a necessary prelude to maturity. Likewise, the materialistic problems described in the previous section are often maximized in a family where the children are so badly needed by one or both parents. Prolonged emotional immaturity is another frequent consequence of overprotection.

I have attempted to show how the extreme approaches to control and love are individually harmful. I should mention another unfortunate circumstance which occurs too often in our society. It is present in homes where the mother and father represent opposing extremes in control. The situation usually follows a familiar pattern: Dad is a very busy man, and he is deeply involved in his work. He is gone from early morning to night, and when he does return, he brings home a briefcase full of work. Perhaps he travels frequently. During the rare times when he is home and not working, he is exhausted. He collapses in front of the TV set to watch a ball game and he doesn't want to be bothered. Consequently, his approach to child control is rather harsh and unsympathetic. His temper flares regularly and the children learn to stay out of his way. By contrast, Mom has no outside world from which to derive personal satisfaction. Her home and her children are her sources of joy; in fact, they have replaced the romantic fires which have vanished from her marriage. She worries about Dad's lack of affection and tenderness for the children. She feels that she should compensate for his sternness by leaning in the other direction.

When he sends the children to bed without their supper, she slips them some milk and cookies. Since she is the only authority on the scene when Dad is gone, the predominant tone in the home is one of unstructured permissiveness. She needs the children too much to risk trying to control them. Thus, the two parental symbols of authority act to contradict each other, and the child is caught somewhere between them. The child respects neither parent because each has assassinated the authority of the other. It has been my observation that these self-destructing forms of authority often load a time-bomb of rebellion that discharges during adolescence. The most hostile, aggressive teen-agers I have known have emerged from this antithetical combination.

The "middle ground" of love and control must be sought if we are to produce healthy, responsible children.

○ ○ ○

THE MIRACLE TOOLS

I n the preceding sections, we dealt with the proper parental response to a child's defiant "challenging behavior." Now we turn our attention to the leadership of children where antagonism is not involved. There are countless situations where the parent wishes to increase the child's level of responsibility, but that task is not easy. How can a mother get her child to brush his teeth regularly, or pick up his clothes, or display table manners? How can she teach him to be more responsible with money? What can the parent do to eliminate obnoxious habits, such as whining, sloppiness, or apparent laziness? Is there a solution to perpetual tardiness? These kinds of behavior do not involve direct confrontations between parent and child, and should not be handled in the same forceful manner described previously. It would be unwise and unfair to punish a youngster for his understandable immaturity and childishness. A much more effective technique is available for use by the knowledgeable parent.

The most magnificent theory ever devised for the control of behavior is called the "Law of Reinforcement," formulated many years ago by the first educational psychologist, E. L. Thorndike. It is magnificent because it works! Thorndike's original law has been honed to a sharp edge of effectiveness by the work of B. F. Skinner, who described the conditions under which the principles work most effectively. Stated simply, the Law of Reinforcement reads, "Behavior which achieves desirable consequences will recur." In other words, if an individual likes what happens as a result of his behavior, he will be inclined to repeat that act. If Sally gets favorable attention from the boys on the day she wears a new dress, she will want to wear the dress again and again. If Pancho wins with one tennis racket and loses with another, he will prefer the racket with which he has found success. This principle is disarmingly simple, but it has profound implications for human learning.

There are specific principles which must be followed if the Law of Reinforcement is to achieve its full potential. Let's consider the elements of this technique in detailed application to children.

1. *Rewards must be granted immediately.* If the maximum effectiveness is to be obtained from a reward, it should be offered shortly after the desirable behavior has occurred. Parents often make the mistake of offering long-range rewards to children, but their successes are few. It is usually unfruitful to offer nine-year-old Joey a car when he is sixteen if he'll work hard in school during the next seven years. Second and third grade elementary children are often promised a trip to grandma's house next summer in exchange for good behavior throughout

the year. Their obedience is typically unaffected by this lure. It is unsatisfactory to offer Mary Lou a new doll for Christmas if she'll keep her room straight in July. Most children have neither the mental capacity nor the maturity to hold a long-range goal in mind day after day. Time moves slowly for them; consequently, the reinforcement seems impossible to reach and uninteresting to contemplate. For animals, a reward should be offered approximately two seconds after the behavior has occurred. A mouse will learn the turns in a maze much faster if the cheese is waiting at the end than he will when a five-second delay is imposed. Although children can tolerate longer delays than animals, the power of a reward is weakened with time.

Immediate reinforcement is the most useful technique available to parents in teaching responsibility to their children. Parents often complain about the irresponsibility of their youngsters, yet they fail to realize that this lack of industriousness has been *learned*. *All* human behavior is learned— the desirable and the undesirable responses. Children learn to laugh, play, run, and jump; they also learn to whine, bully, pout, fight, throw temper tantrums, or be tomboys. The universal teacher is reinforcement. The child repeats the behavior which he considers to be successful. A youngster may be cooperative and helpful because he enjoys the effect that behavior has on his parents; another will sulk and pout for the same reason. When parents recognize characteristics which they dislike in their children, they should set about *teaching* more

35

admirable traits by allowing good behavior to succeed and bad behavior to fail.

Described below are the steps of a program devised by Dr. Malcolm Williamson and myself for use with children between four and six years of age; it can be modified in accordance with the age and maturity of the youngster.

1. The chart on the next page lists some responsibilities and behaviors which the parent may wish to instill. These fourteen items constitute a much greater degree of cooperation and effort than most five-year-old children display on a daily basis, but the proper use of rewards can make it seem more like fun than work. *Immediate* reinforcement is the key: each evening, colored dots (preferably red) or stars should be placed by the behaviors that were done satisfactorily. If dots are not available, the squares can be colored with a felt tip pen; however, the child should be allowed to chalk up his own successes.

2. A penny should be granted for every behavior done properly in a given day; if more than three items are missed in one day, *no* pennies should be given.

3. Since a child can earn a maximum of fourteen cents a day, the parent has an excellent opportunity to teach him how to manage his money. It is suggested that he be allowed to spend only ten to twenty cents per week of these earnings. Special trips to the candy store or toy shop can be planned. The daily ice cream truck provides a handy source of reinforcement. Of the remaining eighty-eight

36

"My Jobs"

November	14	15	16	17	18	19	20	21	22	23	24	25	26	27	28	29	30
1. I brushed my teeth without being told																	
2. I straightened my room before bedtime																	
3. I picked up my clothes without being told																	
4. I fed the fish without being told																	
5. I emptied the trash without being told																	
6. I minded Mommie today..........																	
7. I minded Daddy today																	
8. I said my prayers tonight..........																	
9. I was kind to little brother Billy today																	
10. I took my vitamin pill..........																	
11. I said "thank you" and "please" today..........																	
12. I went to bed last night without complaining																	
13. I gave clean water to the dog today																	
14. I washed my hands and came to the table when called																	
TOTAL:																	

cents (maximum) the child can be required to give ten cents in the church offering or to some other charitable recipient; he should then save about thirty-five cents per week. The final twenty or thirty cents can be accumulated for a long-range expenditure for something he wants or needs.

4. The list of behaviors to be rewarded does *not* remain static. Once the child has got into the habit of hanging up his clothes, or feeding the puppy, or brushing his teeth, the parent should then substitute new responsibilities. A new chart should be made each month, and Junior can make suggestions for his revised chart.

This system provides several side benefits, in addition to the main objective of teaching responsible behavior. Through its use, for example, the child learns to count. He is taught to give to worthy causes. He begins to understand the concept of saving. He learns to restrict and control his emotional impulses. And finally, he is taught the meaning of money and how to spend it wisely. The advantages to his parents are equally impressive. A father of four young children applied the technique and later told me that the noise level in his household had been reduced noticeably.

If this kind of reinforcement is so successful, why has it not been used more widely? The answer to this question is an unfortunate one: adults are reluctant to utilize rewards because they view them as a source of bribery. Our most workable teaching device is ignored because of a philosophical misunderstanding. Our entire society is established on a system of reinforcement, yet we don't want to apply it where it is needed most: with young children. As adults, we go to work each day and receive a pay check on Friday. Getting out of bed each morning is rewarded regularly. Medals are given to brave soldiers; plaques are awarded to successful businessmen; watches are presented to retiring employees. Rewards make responsible effort worthwhile. The main reason for the overwhelming success of capitalism is that hard work and personal discipline are rewarded materially. The great weakness of socialism is the absence of reinforcement; why should a man struggle to achieve if there is nothing special to be gained? The most distasteful aspect of my brief military experience was the absence of reinforcement; I could not get a higher rank until a certain period of time had passed, no matter how hard I worked. The size of my pay check was determined by Congress, not by my competence or output. This system is a destroyer of motivation, yet some parents seem to feel it is the only appropriate one for children. They expect little Marvin to carry responsibility simply because it is noble for him to do so. They want him to work and learn and sweat for the sheer joy of personal discipline. He isn't going to buy it!

Consider the alternative approach to the "bribery" I've recommended. How are *you* going to get your five-year-old to perform the behaviors listed on the chart? The most frequently used substitutes are nagging, complaining, begging, screaming, threatening, and punishing. The mother who objects to the use of rewards may also go to bed each evening with a headache, vowing to have no more children. She didn't like to accentuate materialism in this manner, yet later she will give money to her child. Since her youngster never handles his own cash, he doesn't learn how to save it or spend it wisely. The toys she buys him are purchased with her money, and he values them less. But most important, he is not learning self-discipline and personal responsibility that is possible through the careful reinforcement of that behavior.

I watched the application of these contrasting viewpoints in two actual home situations: Daren's parents felt that he had certain responsibilities as a member of the family. Consequently, he was not rewarded (paid) for his efforts around the home. Daren hated his work because there was no personal gain involved in the effort; it was something to be tolerated. When he had to clean out the garage on Saturday, he would drag himself out to the disaster area and gaze with unfocused eyes at the depressing task before him. As might be expected, he did a miserably poor job because he was absolutely devoid of motivation. This sloppiness brought a tongue-lashing from his dad, which hardly made the experience a pleasant one. Daren's parents were not stingy with him. They supplied his needs and even gave him some spending money; when the State Fair came to town, they would give him $5.00 to spend. Because their gifts were not linked to his responsible efforts, the money provided no source of motivation. Daren grew up hating to work; his parents had inadvertently reinforced his irresponsibility.

Brian's parents took a different view. They felt that he should be paid for the tasks that went beyond his regular household duties. He was not rewarded for carrying out the trash or straightening his room, but he received money for working in the yard on Saturday. This hourly wage was a respectable amount, comparable to what he could earn outside the family. Brian loved his work. He'd get up in the morning and attack the weeds in his backyard; he would count his money and work and look at his watch and work and count his money. At times he rushed home from school to get in an hour or two before dark. He opened his own bank account, and was very careful about how he surrendered his hardearned cash. Brian enjoyed great status in his neighborhood because he always had money in his pocket. He didn't spend it very often, but he *could have done so* at any given moment. That was impressive power! At one point he drew all of his money out of the bank and asked for the total amount in new one dollar bills. He then stacked his twenty-eight bills in his top dresser drawer, and displayed them casually to Daren and his other penniless friends. Work and responsibility were the keys to this status, and he learned a good measure of both. His parents were careful never to give him a cent. They bought his clothes and necessities, but he purchased his own toys and personal indulgences. From an economic point of view, Brian's parents spent no more money than did Daren's mom and dad; they merely linked each penny to the behavior they desired. I believe their approach was the more productive of the two.

As implied before, it is very important to know when to use rewards and when to resort to punishment. It is not recommended that rewards be utilized when the child has challenged the authority of the parent. For example, mom may say, "Come here, Lucy," and Lucy shouts "No!" It is a mistake for mom to then offer a piece of candy if Lucy will comply with her request. She would actually be rewarding her for defiance. If there is still confusion about how to respond in this kind of direct conflict, I suggest the reader take another look at the earlier sections of this book. Rewards should not be used as a substitute for authority; reward and punishment each has its place in child management, and reversals bring unfortunate results.

2. *Rewards need not be material in nature.* When my daughter was three years of age, I began to teach her some pre-reading skills, including the alphabet. By planning the training sessions to occur after dinner each evening, her dessert (bits of chocolate candy) provided the chief source of motivation. Late one afternoon I was sitting on the floor drilling her on several new letters when a tremendous crash shook the neighborhood. The whole family rushed outside immediately to see what had happened, and observed that a teen-ager had wrecked his car on our quiet residential street. The boy was not badly hurt, but his automobile was a mess. We sprayed the smoldering car with water to keep the dripping gas from igniting, and made the necessary phone call to the police. It was not until the excitement began to lessen that we realized our daughter had not followed us out of the house. I returned to the den where I found her elbow deep in the two-pound

bag of candy I had left behind. She had put at least a pound of chocolate into her mouth, and most of the remainder was distributed around her chin, nose, and forehead. When she saw me coming, she managed to jam another handful into her chipmunk cheeks. From this experience, I learned one of the limitations of using material, or at least edible, reinforcement.

Anything that is considered desirable to an individual can serve as reinforcement for his behavior. The most obvious rewards for animals are those which satisfy physical needs, although humans are further motivated to resolve their overwhelming psychological needs. Some children, for example, would rather receive a sincere word of praise than a ten dollar bill, particularly if the adult approval is expressed in front of other children. Children and adults of all ages seek constant sastisfaction of their emotional needs, including the desire for love, social acceptance, and self-respect. Additionally, they hope to find excitement, intellectual stimulation, entertainment, and pleasure.

Most children and adults seek to satisfy their psychological needs from contact with other people. Since we depend on our associates to convince us that we are loved, accepted, and respected, we are keenly interested in what those associates think and say. *As a result, verbal reinforcement can be the strongest motivator of human behavior.* Consider the tremendous impact of the following comments:

"Here comes Phil—the ugliest guy in school."

"Louise is so stupid! She never knows the right answer in class."

"Joe will strike out. He always does."

These unkind assessments burn like acid to the children they describe, causing them to modify future behavior. Phil may become quiet, withdrawn, and easily embarrassed. Louise will probably display even less interest in her schoolwork than before, appearing lazy to her teachers. Joe may give up baseball and other athletic endeavors.

We adults are equally sensitive to the idle comments of our peers. It is often humorous to observe how vulnerable we are to the casual remarks of our friends (and even our enemies). "You've gained a few pounds, haven't you, Martha?" Martha may choose to ignore the comment for the moment, but she will spend fifteen minutes before the mirror that evening and start an extensive diet program the next morning.

"Ralph is about your age, Pete; I'd say he is 46 or 48 years old." Pete is only 39, and the blood drains from his face; the new concern over his appearance may be instrumental in his decision to purchase a toupee the following month.

Our hearing apparatus is more attuned to this kind of personal evaluation than any other subject, and our sense of self-respect and worthiness emerge largely from these unintentional messages.

Despite our dependence on social feedback, we are surprisingly unaware of the degree to which we influence those around us. The next time the reader is involved in a three-way discussion, I suggest that he pause to observe the other participant who is not talking at the moment. With few exceptions, that listener will not be standing immobile and passive. He will probably be providing the talker with a steady stream of information, revealing how the spoken ideas are being received. As the talker rambles on, the listener is nodding his head, smiling in agreement, mumbling "Uh-huh" and "Yes, that's true." Or he may be expressing disagreement in a similar gesturing fashion. The talker is anything but immune to this evaluation of his thoughts; he sees the cues and alters his conversation accordingly. Enthusiastic responses from the listener will produce more excitement in the talker. If he is speaking on a controversial topic or a subject with which he is uneasy, he may "fish" for additional reinforcement, saying, "Haven't you found that true, Jack?" The listener then becomes the talker, and the feedback is provided to him in reverse. Social behavior is highly dependent on this kind of verbal reinforcement, occurring in everyday conversation. The same is true in the relationship between the parent and child, and the astute parent will capitalize on this pleasant source of motivation.

Verbal reinforcement should permeate the entire parent-child relationship. Too often our parental instruction consists of a million "don'ts" which are jammed down the child's throat. We should spend more time rewarding him for the behavior we do admire, even if our "reward" is nothing more than a sincere compliment. Remembering the child's need for self-esteem and acceptance, the wise parent can satisfy those important longings while using them to teach valued concepts and behavior. A few examples may be helpful:

Mother to daughter: You certainly colored nicely within the lines on that picture, Rene. I like to see that kind of neat art work. I'm going to put this on the bulletin board in the hall.

Mother to husband in son's presence: Jack, did you notice how Don put his bicycle in the garage tonight? He used to leave it out until we told him to put it away; he is becoming much more responsible, don't you think?

Father to son: I appreciate your being quiet while I was figuring the income tax, son. You were very thoughtful. Now that I have that job done, I'll have more time. Why don't we plan to go to the zoo next Saturday?

Teacher to high school student: You've made a good point, Juan. I hadn't thought of that aspect of the matter. I enjoy your original way of looking at things.

Mother to small son: Kevin, you haven't sucked your thumb all morning. I'm very proud of you. Let's see how long you can go this afternoon.

It is unwise for a parent to compliment the child for behavior she does not admire. If everything the child does earns him a big hug and a pat on the back, Mom's approval gradually becomes meaningless. Inflation can destroy the value of her reinforcement. Specific behavior warranting genuine compliments can be found if it is sought, even in the most mischievous youngster.

3. *Any behavior which is learned through reinforcement can be eliminated if the reward is withheld long enough.*

It is an absolute fact that unreinforced behavior will eventually disappear. This process, called *extinction* by psychologists, can be very useful to parents and teachers who want to alter the characteristics of children. The animal world provides many interesting examples of extinction; for example, the wall-eyed pike is a large fish with a big appetite for minnows. If he is placed in a tank of water with his small colleagues, he will soon be in the tank alone. However, an interesting thing occurs when a plate of glass is slipped down the middle of the tank, separating the pike from the minnows. The pike cannot see the glass, and he hits it solidly in pursuit of his dinner. Again and again he will swim into the glass, bumping whatever one calls the front end of a wall-eyed pike. His behavior is *not* being reinforced; it is gradually being extinguished. Eventually, the pike gives up in discouragement. He has learned that it is not possible to get the minnows. The glass can then be taken from the tank, allowing the minnows to swim around their mortal enemy in perfect safety. He will not try to eat them. He knows what he knows. They are unreachable. The wall-eyed pike will actually starve to death while his favorite food is bumping him on the gills and mouth.

Extinction is utilized to prevent circus elephants from throwing their mighty power against the restraining chain each evening. When the elephant is young, his foot is chained to a cement block that is totally immovable. He will pull repeatedly against the barrier without success, thereby extinguishing his escape behavior. Later a small rope and a fragile stake will be sufficient to restrain the powerful elephant.

In order to eliminate an undesirable behavior, one must identify and then withhold the critical reinforcement. Let's apply this principle to a common childhood problem: why does a child whine instead of speaking in a normal voice? Because the parent has reinforced whining! As long as three-year-old Karen is speaking in her usual voice, her mom is too busy to listen to her. Karen babbles all day long, anyway, so her mother tunes out most of her verbiage. But when Karen speaks in a grating, irritating, obnoxious tone, her mom turns to see what is wrong. Karen's whining brings results; her normal voice does not: she becomes a whiner. In order to extinguish the whining, one must merely reverse the reinforcement. Mom should begin by saying, "I can't hear you because you're whining, Karen. I have funny ears; they just can't hear whining." After this message has been passed along for a day or two, Mom should show no indication of having heard a moan-tone. She should then offer immediate attention to a request made in a normal voice. If this control of reinforcement is applied properly, I guarantee it to achieve the desired results. All learning is based on this principle, and the consequences are certain and definite. Of course, Grandma and Uncle Albert may continue to reinforce the behavior you are trying to extinguish, and they can keep it alive.

Teachers should know how to tame the classroom show-off in the same manner. First decide

48

what is motivating his behavior: it takes no great scientist to recognize that the loudmouth is usually seeking the attention of the group. Some children had much rather be thought of as obnoxious than to be unthought of at all. For them, anonymity is the most painful experience imaginable. The ideal prescription is to extinguish their attention-getting behavior and then meet their need for gaining acceptance by less noisy means. I worked with a giddy little sixth grader named Larry whose mouth never shut. He perpetually disrupted the tranquility of his class, setting up a constant barrage of silliness, wise remarks and horseplay. His teacher and I constructed an isolated area in a remote corner of the schoolroom; from that spot he could see nothing but the front of the room. Thereafter, Larry was sentenced to a week in the isolation booth whenever he chose to be disruptive, which effectively eliminated the supporting reinforcement. Certainly, he could still act silly behind the screen, but he could not see the effect he was having on his peers. Besides this limitation, each outburst lengthened his lonely isolation. Larry spent one entire month in relative solitude before the extinction was finalized. When he rejoined society, his teacher immediately began to reward his cooperation. He was given the high status jobs (messenger, sergeant-at-arms, etc.) and praised for the improvement he had made. The results were remarkable.

Extinction occasionally happens accidentally, as it did in the case of four-year-old Mark. His mother and father were concerned about his irritating habit of throwing temper tantrums. He would select the time when his parents least wanted him to misbehave; when guests were visiting in their home, he could be expected to explode at bedtime, if not before. Mark repeated the same emotional performance in restaurants, church services and other public places. His parents were no strangers to discipline, and they unloaded all their resources on their little rebel. They spanked him, stood him in the corner, sent him to bed early, shamed and scolded him. Nothing worked. The temper tantrums continued on a regular basis. Finally, they reached the point of exasperation. They didn't know what else to do. Then one evening Mark's parents were reading the newspaper in their living room. They had said something that angered him, and he fell on the floor in a rage. He screamed and whacked his head on the carpet, kicking, and flailing his small arms. They didn't know what to do with him, so they did nothing. They went on reading the paper. That reaction was totally unexpected by villainous Mark. He got up, looked at his father, and fell down for Act II. Again his parents made no response. Mark's yelling stopped abruptly. He went over to his mother and shook her arm, then collapsed for Act III. Still they made no move toward him. He apparently felt so silly flopping alone on the floor that he never threw another tantrum. In retrospect, it is clear that the reinforcement for Mark's tantrums was parental manipulation. He was able to get those big, powerful adults upset and distraught through this violent behavior. Tantrums are more frequently a form of challenging behavior which can be eliminated by one or more appropriate spankings; for a few children, like Mark, the spanking itself is actually a form of reinforcement. For Mark, like the pyromaniac, it was rewarding to see how much commotion he could precipitate.

Although Mark's parents extinguished his negative behavior in one episode, it usually takes much longer. It is important to understand the typical rate at which a characteristic will disappear without reinforcement. Consider the example of a pigeon checking radio tubes. He began the learning exercise by missing all the defective tubes, gradually recognizing a higher and higher percentage. As is illustrated in Figure A, the pigeon eventually identified one hundred percent of the tubes, and he continued to function with perfect accuracy as long as the reinforcement (grain) was paid for each success. Suppose the reinforcement was then withheld. The pigeon would continue to intercept the defective parts with perfect accuracy, but not for long. Soon he would begin to miss a few tubes. If he continued to work for nothing, he would become more and more distracted and disinterested in his task. By the end of the day, he would miss all or most of the defective tubes. However, the following day, he would again go to work as before. *Even though the behavior is extinguished on one day, it is likely to return the next.* This reawakening is called "spontaneous recovery." Each day the behavior returns as illustrated in Figure B, but the accuracy is less and the daily extinction occurs more quickly than the day before. This principle is important in the extinction of undesirable behavior

51

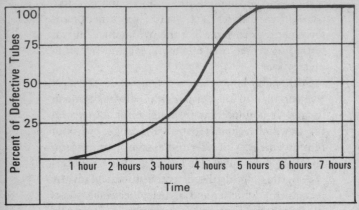

Figure A

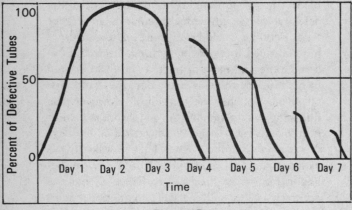

Figure B

in children. A parent or teacher should not become discouraged if an extinguished behavior continues to reappear. The complete process of eliminating a response may require a considerable period of time.

Extinction can be useful in helping the child overcome some of his unnecessary fears. I consulted with a mother who was very worried about her three-year-old daughter's fear of the dark. Despite the use of a night light and leaving the bedroom door open, Marla was afraid to stay in her room alone. She insisted that her mother sit with her until she went to sleep each evening, which became very time-consuming and inconvenient. If Marla happened to awaken in the night, she would call for help. It was apparent that the child was not bluffing; she was genuinely frightened. Fears such as this are not innate characteristics in the child; they have been learned. Parents must be very careful in expressing their fears, because their youngsters are amazingly perceptive in adopting those same concerns. For that matter, good-natured teasing can also produce problems for a child. If a youngster walks into a dark room and is pounced upon from behind the door, he has learned something from the joke: the dark is not always empty! In Marla's case, it is unclear where she learned to fear the dark, but I believe her mother inadvertently magnified the problem. In her concern for Marla, she conveyed her anxiety, and Marla began to think that her fears must be justified. "Even mother is worried about it." The fright became so great that Marla could not walk through a dimly lit room without an escort. It was at this point that the child was referred to me. I suggested that the mother tell Marla she was going to help her see that there was nothing to be afraid of. (It is usually unfruitful to try to *talk* a child out of his fears, but it helps to show him you are confident and unthreatened.) She bought a bag of candy and placed her chair just outside Marla's bedroom door. Marla was then offered a piece of candy if she could spend a short time (ten seconds) in her bedroom with the light on and the door shut. This first step was not very threatening, and Marla enjoyed the game. It was repeated several times; then she was asked to walk a few feet into the darkened room with the door open while mother (clearly visible in the hall) counted to ten. Marla accomplished this task several times and was given the candy on each occasion. On subsequent trips, the door was shut halfway, followed by a more narrow opening. Finally, Marla had the courage to enter the dark room and shut the door while her mother counted to ten. She knew she could come out immediately if she wished. Mother talked confidently and quietly. The length of time in the dark was gradually lengthened, and instead of producing fear, it produced candy: ultimate pleasure to a small child. Courage was being reinforced; fear was being extinguished. The cycle of fright was thereby broken, being replaced by a more healthy attitude.

The uses of extinction are limited only by the imagination and creativity of the parent or teacher. The best method of changing a behavior is to withhold its reinforcement while rewarding its replacement.

4. Parents and teachers are also vulnerable to reinforcement. Reinforcement is not only the mechanism by which children and animals learn new behavior; adults also modify their behavior according to their successes and failures. Not infrequently a child will train his parents, rather than the reverse, by reinforcing certain behaviors and extinguishing others. A few examples are described below:

When Mother and Father decide to take their children to some exciting place, such as Disneyland, the youngsters put on their best behavior. They are sweet and cooperative, in an unsubtle attempt to "reinforce" their parents' behavior. In extreme cases, I have seen children manipulate their parents in a cool application of reinforcement to the behavior they prefer.

When Mom disciplines her eight-year-old daughter, the child says, "You don't love me anymore." Most children know their parents are anxious to convey their love, so they use this delicate issue to extinguish punishment. It often succeeds.

When the teacher says, "It is time to study health, so get out your health books," the entire class groans "Oh, no!" For some teachers, this lack of reinforcement is very difficult to tolerate, and the subject of health is eliminated from their curriculum in the future. Similar phenomena occur in higher education too! I knew of a graduate school psychology class which was studying the principles of reinforcement, and the students decided to conduct an experiment involving their professor. Their instructor utilized two approaches to teaching: he would lecture from his notes, which proved to be a dry, dismal experience for the students. However, he was much more interesting when they could get him to talk extemporaneously, answering their questions and speaking from his wealth of knowledge. The students agreed before class one day to reward his free conversation and extinguish his formal lecturing behavior. Whenever he talked from his notes, they shuffled their feet, looked out the window, yawned and whispered to each other. On the other hand, they reflected maximum fascination with his unstructured lessons. The professor responded in classic fashion: Although he did not know he was being manipulated until near the end of the semester, he changed his mode of instruction in favor of the informal approach.

Father has a very low frustration tolerance with his children. Whenever they fall short of his expectations, he yells at them, which seems to make them mind. He has been reinforced for his screaming and becomes a loud, aggressive parent.

Adults even reinforce each other in regard to the subjects about which they will converse. For example, Marsha and Harry are talking but Harry is bored with the topic; for that matter, Harry is also bored with Marsha. His disinterest cannot be concealed. His boredom produces telltale yawns that defy suppression. They creep up Harry's throat and pound on his teeth until released. Harry waits until Marsha looks away, then he sets his jaw, swallows hard, and squeezes the yawn out his eyes. When Marsha looks at Harry again, she sees suspicious tears left by the compressed yawn. Marsha can hardly miss the other signs of boredom, including

Harry's lack of involvement and his glazed appearance. Perhaps without conscious awareness, Marsha knows she isn't impressing Harry; she may terminate the conversation as quickly as possible, or at least change the topic. Unless she is socially dead, she will decode and react to the lack of reinforcement Harry is providing. In a similar fashion, we "tell" each other what subjects we want to talk about.

The point of this section is simple: parents should be aware of their own reactions to reinforcement, and make certain they are in control of the new learning situation.

5. *Parents often reinforce undesirable behavior and weaken the behavior they value.* Perhaps the most important aspect of this section relates to accidental reinforcement. It is remarkably easy to reward undesirable behavior in children by allowing it to succeed. Suppose, for example, that Mr. and Mrs. Weakknee are having guests in for dinner tonight, and they put three-year-old Ricky to bed at 7:00 P.M. They know Ricky will cry, as he always does, but what else can they do? Indeed, Ricky cries. He begins at a low pitch (which does not succeed) and gradually builds to a high intensity scream. Finally, Mrs. Weakknee becomes so embarrassed by the display that she lets Ricky get up. What has the child learned? That he must cry loudly if he wants to get up. Mr. and Mrs. Weakknee had better be prepared for a tearful battle scene tomorrow night, too, because the method was successful to Ricky the night before.

Betty Sue is an argumentative teen-ager. She never takes "no" for an answer. She is very cantakerous; in fact, her father says the only time she is every homesick is when she is at home. Whenever her mother is not sure about whether she wants to let Betty go to a party or ball game, she will first tell her she *can't* go. By saying an initial "no," Betty's mom doesn't commit herself to a "yes" before she's had a chance to think it over. She can always change her mind from negative to positive, but it is difficult to go the other way. However, what does this system tell Betty? She can see that "no" really means "maybe." The harder she argues and complains, the more likely she is to obtain the desired "yes." Many parents make the same mistake as Betty Sue's mother. They allow arguing, sulking, pouting, door-slamming, and bargaining to succeed. A parent should not take a definitive position on an issue until he has thought it over thoroughly. Then he should stick tenaciously to his stand. If the teen-ager learns that "no" means "absolutely no," he is less likely to waste his effort appealing his case to higher courts.

Seven-year-old Abe wants the attention of his family, and he knows of no constructive way to get it. At the dinner table one evening his mother says, "Eat your beans, Abe," to which he replies defiantly, "No! I won't eat those rotten beans!" He has the eyes and ears of the whole family—something he wanted in the first place. Abe's mother can solidify the success of his defiance (and guarantee its return) by saying, "If you'll eat your beans I'll give you a treat."

The crying of infants is an important form of communication. Through their tears we learn of their hunger, fatigue, discomfort, or diaper disaster. Although we do not want to eliminate crying in babies, it is possible to make them less fussy and tearful by minimizing the reinforcement of this behavior. If an infant is immediately picked up or rocked each time he cries, he may quickly observe the relationship between tears and adult attention. I have stood at the doorway of my daughter's nursery for four or five minutes, awaiting a momentary lull in the crying before going to her crib. By so doing, I reinforce the pauses rather than the emotional intensity.

Obviously, a parent must be careful in the behavior he allows to succeed. He must exercise self-discipline and patience to insure that the reinforcement which takes place is positive, not negative in its results.

Summary

Lest I be misunderstood, I shall emphasize my message by stating its opposite. I am not recommending that your home be harsh and oppressive. I am not suggesting that you give your children a spanking every morning with their ham and eggs, or that you make your boys sit in the living room with their hands folded and their legs crossed. (Children are like clocks; they must be allowed to run.) I am not proposing that you try to make adults out of your little children so you can impress your adult friends with your parental skill, or that you punish your

59

children whimsically, swinging and screaming when they didn't know they were wrong. I am not suggesting that you insulate your dignity and authority by being cold and unapproachable. These parental tactics do not produce healthy, responsible children. By contrast, I am recommending a simple principle: when you are defiantly challenged, win decisively. When the child asks, "Who's in charge?" tell him. When he mutters, "Who loves me?" take him in your arms and surround him with affection. Treat him with respect and dignity, and expect the same from him. Then begin to enjoy the sweet benefits of competent parenthood.

◦ ◦ ◦

OTHER MATERIALS FOR THE FAMILY
BY DR. JAMES DOBSON

Books:

Dare to Discipline, Tyndale House Publishers, 1970. (Over one million copies of this text have been sold.)

Hide or Seek, Self-Esteem for the Child, Fleming H. Revell Publishing Company, 1974.

The Mentally Retarded Child and His Family, Brunner-Mazel Publishers, 1970. (This book was co-edited with Dr. Richard Koch.)

What Wives Wish Their Husbands Knew About Women, Tyndale House Publishers, 1975.

Cassette Tape Recordings:

Dare to Discipline, Vision House Publishers (One Way Library). This album contains six cassette tapes, based on the concepts discussed in the book by the same name.

Preparing for Adolescence, Vision House Publishers (One Way Library). This album contains six cassette tapes, designed to help the preteen-ager prepare for the experience to come.

Self-Esteem for the Child, Vision House Publishers

(One Way Library). This album contains four cassette tapes, and presents the ways parents and teachers can maximize self-confidence in children.

What Wives Wish Their Husbands Knew About Women, Vision House Publishers (One Way Library). This album deals with the basic content of the book by the same name although it contains speeches, radio interviews, and counseling conversations. Dr. Dobson has called this album, "The most important work of my professional life."

These items are available in local bookstores, or can be ordered by writing Box 952, Temple City, California 91780. Dr. Dobson can also be contacted through that address, although he regrets that he is unable to respond to requests for personal consultation.